Northwest Arkansas Travel Guide

Insider Secrets

Anna Seeger

PUBLISHED BY
Lanie Dills Publishing
Copyright © 2012
ISBN 9780916744045

All rights reserved: No part of this publication may be replicated, redistributed, or given away in any form without prior written consent of the author/publisher or terms relayed to you herein.

For Don & Becky
They Made Northwest Arkansas A Better Place

- Introduction 5
- Getting To NWA 5
- Transportation 6
- Driving - How Far Away Is NWA? 6
- Bentonville 7
  - What the Locals Say… 8
  - Arts 10
  - Dining In Bentonville 13
  - Entertainment 16
  - Festivals 17
  - Hotels In Bentonville 18
  - Museums 19
  - Recreation 21
  - Hiking – Biking Trails… 21
  - Mountain Biking Trails 22
- Bella Vista 23
  - Dining 23
  - Theatre 23
  - Museums 24
  - Outdoor Recreation 25
  - Golf – 8 Golf Courses 25
  - Lakes 29
  - Festivals 31
  - Bella Vista Arts & Crafts Festival 31
- Eureka Springs 32
  - What the Locals Say… 33
  - Arts 35
  - Dining In Eureka Springs 37
  - Day Entertainment 39
  - Hotels In Eureka Springs 42
  - Nightlife & Entertainment 44
  - Recreation 46
  - Shopping 50
- Fayetteville 52
  - What the Locals Say… 53
  - Arts 55

- Dining In Fayetteville 58
- Festivals 63
- Hotels In Fayetteville 64
- Museums 65
- Nightlife/Entertainment 69
- Theatres 69
- Shopping 71
- Sports & Recreation In Fayetteville 73
- Golf 75
- Hiking, Biking & Camping 75

Lowell 78
- Dining 78
- Outdoor Recreation 78

Rogers 79
- What the Locals Say… 79
- Arts 81
- Dining In Rogers 82
- Festivals 85
- Hotels In Rogers 86
- Museums 87
- Outdoor Recreation 89
- Lakes 89
- Golf 90
- Parks 90
- Shopping 93

Springdale 96
- Arts 97
- Dining in Springdale 98
- Hotels in Springdale 99
- Sports & Recreation 100

Introduction

The Northwest corner of Arkansas is home to a number of towns and many smaller communities, which together are commonly referred to as Northwest Arkansas (NWA). Bentonville, Bella Vista, Eureka Springs, Fayetteville, Rogers and Springdale are the towns covered in this quick guide to the area.

This unique picturesque area has many facets, some simple and some complex and sophisticated. Always noted for its natural beauty and clean mountain air, it has grown to encompass an enormous variety of attractions. What you will find in NWA is a friendly area with a fascinating history and a thriving business community. Who could have imagined that Wal-Mart, the largest corporation in the world, would incubate and establish itself using this tiny corner of the state as its base.

While it is still the headquarters for Wal-Mart, NWA is also the home of the Crystal Bridges American Art Museum, a retirement village, a championship college sports program, metropolitan shopping, a quaint Victorian village, exciting unique nightlife, posh accommodations, championship golf; and, in recent years, it has gone through a metamorphosis to the extent that anyone can find a long list of many different activities to enjoy.

Getting To NWA

The NWA airport is referred to as XNA and while it is located in Bentonville. It serves all the communities of Northwest Arkansas. It is small enough so you don't spend hours getting in and out and yet large enough you can fly to just about anywhere from XNA.

Since Southwest airlines flies in and out of Tulsa, you can opt to fly in to Tulsa. Tulsa is about one and a half to two hours away from Bentonville. Not a bad drive, but XNA is far easier and quicker.

Transportation

NWA is still in its infancy as far as mass transportation is concerned. You will need to have a car to travel around town as well as from city to city. Fortunately, there are many rental car companies located at both airports and in town, however, during the week of the Wal-Mart stock holders meeting, the big arts and crafts weeks and other festivals, it is wise to book your transportation well in advance.

Driving - How Far Away Is NWA?

Albuquerque, New Mexico 704 miles approximately 11 hours
Branson, Missouri 93 miles approximately 1 hour 45 min.
Dallas, Texas 398 miles approximately 6 hours
Irvine, California 1554 miles approximately 24 hours
Kansas City, Missouri 268 miles –approximately 3 hours 30 min.
Kingwood, Texas 463 miles approximately 8 hours
Little Rock, Arkansas 203 miles approximately 3 hours 15 min.
Memphis, Tennessee 336 miles approximately 5 hours 30 min.
Oklahoma City, Oklahoma 225 miles approximately 3 hours 45 min.
St. Louis, Missouri 329 miles approximately 5 hours
Tulsa, Oklahoma 118 miles approximately 2 hours

Bentonville

Bentonville is an epitome of opposites. This town of 36,000 and rapidly growing is the home to Wal-Mart Stores, Inc. Yes, the largest retailer in the world made and has kept its home office in Bentonville, a most unlikely place. Headquarters for businesses even half this size are, typically, reserved for cities like New York, Los Angeles and Chicago.

It isn't uncommon to be standing in line at the local Bentonville Wal-Mart store with the buyer of bedding, sporting goods, women's apparel or jewelry. These buyers and other head buyers are responsible for spending billions of dollars worldwide, but when you live in Bentonville, they are everyday people and could be just your next-door neighbor or maybe one of your relatives that happens to be employed by the big-box retailing giant.

Likewise, as a visitor to Bentonville, you could be eating your dinner right next to one of the Wal-Mart top executives and never know it. Wal-Mart is not only a force throughout the world, but it also has a tremendous impact on its own hometown.

Another unlikely entity found in Bentonville is the new world-renowned Crystal Bridges Museum of American Art. The museum was founded largely through the efforts and financial support of Alice Walton, the youngest heir to the Wal-Mart fortune.

Crystal Bridges has almost instantly joined the ranks of some of the richest museums in the country with an endowment of $800 million by the Walton Family Foundation. Though opened only since November of 2011, it already ranks among the top museums in the world. Of course, museums of this stature are typically located in New York, Los Angeles, Washington and Chicago and not in the bedrock of Middle America.

The magnificent structure that houses the art is regarded as an architectural masterpiece. The museum's glass-and-wood design with its gently curving pavilions is nestled around two spring-fed ponds. Designed by Moshe Safdie, it is regarded as America's newest cultural institution.

Bentonville, until the recent Crystal Bridges opening in 2011 retained its small town feel, but has since morphed into a town that has a trendy downtown square littered with independent upscale restaurants, shops. Soon, the 21c Museum Hotel will open to accommodate visitors from around the country and the globe. 21c promises a special combination of hotel and art and is located close to Crystal Bridges.

Galleries and hotels are popping up throughout the area. Hotels, offering every amenity imaginable, are already plentiful, but the 21c will, no doubt, be the ultimate in hotel experience.

There are many numerous hiking and biking trails around the downtown and museum areas. Have a bite to eat at one of the old or new sumptuous restaurants and then take a leisurely stroll around the quaint and beautiful town square.

What the Locals Say…

The Crystal Bridges Museum of American Art - Of course, the big can't miss thing to see is Crystal Bridges, you don't have to be a professional artist or an art critic in order to enjoy the incredible magnificence of this museum.

The Wal-Mart Visitor Center – Everyone should see this fascinating center. You don't have to be a big fan of Wal-Mart to appreciate the size and scope of this worldwide mega corporation. See the history of Wal-Mart and its founders in this interactive museum center.

Wal-Mart - Another treat is to actually visit the Wal-Mart store in Bentonville. You won't ever have a better experience at a Wal-Mart than you will at the store in Wal-Mart's hometown.

Can't Miss Restaurants – The locals have their favorites like: The Station Café (best burgers around), Table Mesa, Fred's Hickory Inn, The Red Onion and The River Grille. The Pressroom for coffee and breakfast is an excellent choice.

Bentonville Square - The Downtown area referred to as the Bentonville Square is something unique and continues to get better and better. First Friday on the square occurs on the Bentonville Square on the first Friday of every month, usually with some kind of theme. Vendor booths are set up all over the square. There are free food samples, live music, lots of unique stuff and a lively crowd. During this time, you can't actually drive around the square. Dining at the downtown restaurants is also available.

Farmers Market downtown Saturday mornings during the spring/summer is a great place to pick up fresh vegetables. Phat Tire is a terrific bike shop that is very helpful and even rents bicycles out.

Bentonville Hiking and Biking Trails - The hiking and biking trails in Bentonville are second to none. Bentonville is the host for 2014 International Mountain Biking Association Summit.

Last but not least if you would like additional information on Bentonville, be sure to check out the Bentonville Convention and Visitors Bureau (http://bentonvilleusa.org). They have a wealth of information about different upcoming events.

Arts

Image credit Arkansas.com

Crystal Bridges Museum of American Art
600 Museum Way
Bentonville, AR
Phone (479) 418-5700

Named for the natural spring that feeds the Museum's two ponds and the unusual bridge construction that is a part of the overall design, Crystal Bridges, saw more than 160 thousand worldwide visitors within the first 4 ½ months of its opening.

Moshe Safdie, the designer, was selected not only for his commitment to the use of social, cultural and geographic elements that elucidate an area, but also for his designs that respond to human needs and goals.

The 120-acre museum park features six galleries, restaurant, research library, sculpture trail, classrooms and grand hall for special events.

American art from five centuries is represented here including works by John Singleton Copley, Winslow Homer, Thomas Eakins, Andy Warhol and Georgia O'Keeffe.
Cost of admission is free.

Studio 124
Thomas B. Merrit Studio Gallery
Midtown Shopping Center
Bentonville, AR 72712
Phone (479) 263-6338

Art
By Becky Christenson
2204 S.E. 14th Street
Bentonville, Arkansas 72712
Phone (479) 273-0668

Art features the work of artist Becky Christenson who specializes in one-of-a-kind designs…including sculptures, paintings, ceramics and other original works.

Big Red Gallery
Rich & Sandra Anderson
Larry & Sherri Rice
9400 East McNelly Road
Bentonville, AR 72712
Phone: (479) 451- 8866

Proudly offering their customers the largest selection of Limited Edition Prints, Limited Edition Canvas', Limited Edition Giclee', Canvas' and Originals in Northwest Arkansas.

Art Seen 107 Gallery
107 S. E. Third St.

Bentonville, AR
Phone (479) 619-9115

Gallery featuring contemporary art.

Arend Arts Center
Live on Stage
1901 SE J Street
Bentonville, AR
Phone (479) 254-5161

A part of the Bentonville Public School System, the Arend Arts Center is an important center for both school and community arts in NWA. The Benton County Symphony performs there annually as do many professional artists like pianists Vladimir Zaitsey and Rosario Andino.

Dining In Bentonville

Fine Dining
Table Mesa Bentonville (Bistro)
River Grille Bentonville Ar - the River grill
Doe's Eat Place
Fred's Hickory Inn
Tusk & Trotter
Petit Bistro

Casual Dining
American
The Station Cafe
Hapa's Hawaiian Grill
Wing Stop
Buffalo Wild Wings
Ruby Tuesday Restaurants
Bud's Family- Style Chicken
Ron's Hamburgers & Chilli
Beef-O-Brady's
Flying Fish

Asian
Mama's Fu's Asian House
Sushi House
Thai Kitchen
Sho-Gun
Gold Town Sushi & Korean BBQ
Li's Home Cooking Chinese Cuisine

Bakery
Jack's Bakery
Bizzy B's Bakery

BBQ
Dink's Pit Barbeque
Smokin' Joe's Ribhouse
Whole Hog Cafe

13

[Big Rub BBQ](#)

Breakfast
[Antrim's Pancake House](#)
[Pressroom](#)
[Red Onion Espressoria](#)
[The Station Cafe](#)
[Village Inn](#)
[Denny's](#)

Buffet
[Lin's Garden Chinese Restaurant](#)
[Orlando's Place](#)

Coffee Houses
[Caffinity](#)
[Kennedy Coffee Roasting Company](#)
[Le Barista Coffee](#)
[Starbucks](#)
[Pressroom](#)

Greek & Mediterranean
[Zary's Acropolis Restaurant](#)

Indian
[India Orchard](#)
[Kobe Sushi and Grill](#)
[A Taste of Thai II](#)
[Aroma](#)
[Taj Indian Cuisine](#)

Italian
Metro Italiano

Mexican
[Las Fajita's Mexican Grill](#)
[Glasgow's](#)
[Acambaro Mexican Restaurant](#)
[Sabores](#)

Los zarapes

Sandwich Shops
Red Onion Espressoria
Panera Bread
Jimmy John's Gourmet Subs
Honeybaked Ham & Cafe
Crumpet Tea Room Express
Flying Burrito
Lenny's Sub Shop
McAlister's Deli
Cheesecake Etc

Pizza
Gusano's Chicago-Style Pizzeria
Jim's Razorback Pizza
Johnny Brusco's New York Style Pizza

Entertainment

Downtown Bentonville on the Square

The downtown square is the central hub of activities. There are popular restaurants that line the square and the surrounding area. An old favorite, "The Station Café", serves the best hamburger in NWA. Flying Fish, Tavola, Tusk and Trotter, Table Mesa and Pressroom are all upscale restaurants that serve delicious food in unique cozy environments.

There are also mobile eateries that are available on the square for special events. These aren't your typical hot dog stands. You won't believe some of the taste-treat delights that are in store for you when you sample some of the delicious foods from such vendors as Crepes Paulette, Big Rub BBQ and Greenhouse Grill.

Additional Restaurants

There are restaurants throughout town, such as The River Grill where exceptional chefs create a different sumptuous special for you to taste every night. For outstanding hickory smoked pit barbecue meals, Fred's Hickory Inn is the place to go. And there are many other delightful restaurants especially along Walton Blvd.

Festivals

County Fairs

Benton and Washington County Fairs are held from mid to late August every year. The Fairs are a true fall tradition and are enjoyed for their livestock shows, fair foods, special events and rides.

Arts & Crafts Events

Festivals and Arts and Crafts are a big deal in NWA. The various events attract more than 250,000 crafts enthusiasts from all over the country. Festivals include: Long's Old Orchard & Farm Arts & Crafts Festival, Ole Applegate Place Autumn Arts & Crafts Festival, Ozark Regional Arts &Crafts Show, Rogers Antique Show & Sale, Rogers Expo Center, Sharp's Show of War Eagle, Spanker Creek Farm Arts & Crafts, War Eagle Fair, War Eagle Mill Antique & Crafts Show, Bella Vista Arts & Crafts, Craft Fair Around the Square, Frisco Station Mall Arts & Crafts, Hillbilly Corner and the Jones Center Arts & Crafts.

Hotels In Bentonville

Luxury Accommodations

Doubletree Bentonville AR – Suites by Hilton Hotels
TownePlace Suites by Mariott
Courtyard By Marriott – Bentonville
Simmons Suites
21 C – Opening 1st Quarter of 2013
Springhill Suites
Hilton Garden Inn Bentonville
Wingate by Wyndham

Mid-Range Accommodations

Best Western Plus Castlerock
Laquinta Inn & Suites
Comfort Suite
Days Inn
Econo Lodge
Holiday Inn Express Hotel & Suites
Travelodge
Super 8

Extended Stay Accommodations

South Walton Suites – Spa
Surburban Extended Stay Hotel
Value Place Extended Stay
Microtel

Bed & Breakfast

The Inn at Bella Vista
Hidden Valley Inn
Laughlin House

Museums

Image credit Arkansas.com

The Wal-Mart Visitors Center
105 North Main
Bentonville, AR
Phone (479) 273-1329

Located on the town square in Bentonville in Sam Walton's original variety store, the Visitors Center details history of the Wal-Mart family particularly Sam Walton, the founder of Wal-Mart and the historic rise of the big-box retailer on the world's stage. It features interactive displays and one-of-a-kind exhibits.

Wal-Mart employees and other visitors from all across the country have a wonderful place to discover the history of Wal-Mart and its founder. It's an interesting and fun activity for families to enjoy.

The Museum of Native American History
202 S.W. "O" Street

Bentonville, AR
Phone (479) 273-2456

View America's past, visit one of south's most comprehensive collections of Native American Artifacts. Make a point to see this unique museum while in the area.

[1875 Peel Mansion & Heritage Gardens](#)
400 South Walton Boulevard
Bentonville, AR
Phone (479) 273-9664

The Peel Mansion and Heritage Gardens built by Colonel Samuel West Peel and his wife Mary Emaline Berry Peel is a wonderful example of a Civil War era home. It is available for tours and events.

Recreation

Hiking – Biking Trails…

Image Credit J. Scott

Bentonville Trail System

The Bentonville Trail system is made up of three looped trails that connect and meander through three beautiful parks including Lake Bella Vista, Memorial Park and Park Springs Park. There are also seven linear bikeways and pedestrian paths. For the mountain bikers, there is an all-terrain bike trail. Additionally, there are numerous on-road bike routes. In all there is a network amounting to over 20 trail miles.

The Crystal Bridges Trail

Along the western edge of the Crystal Bridges 120 acre museum park is a beautiful shaded multi-use trail. 1.5 miles long, the trail meanders along stunning sculpture and there is also an overlook to the Crystal Bridges Museum of American Art.

Compton Gardens and Conference Center
The home was the home of Dr. Neil Compton who passed away in 1999. Credited with saving the Buffalo National River, he was an avid naturalist and a local physician. The grounds around the home are now a beautiful 6.5-acre park composed of native woodland gardens. Today, the home/conference center is available for events, meetings, seminars, retreats, film and photo shoots and tours.

Park Springs (Funky Town)
Traveling through natural wooded areas is the North Bentonville Trail. The trailhead is located at 2400 North Walton Blvd. and is composed of a 10' wide concrete linear trail and a jogging path, which is along side the linear trail. Parking and restrooms are available at the trailhead.

Mountain Biking Trails

Slaughter Pen Mountain Bike Trail
5.18 miles long and designed especially for mountain bike enthusiasts, it is located on the mountainside just north of northwest "A" St.; Slaughter Pen is an unusual and sometimes challenging single-track trail.

Special features of Slaughter Pen include drops, jumps, log rides and there is also a free ride area that includes a wall ride, table top jumps and bermed turns. There is a trail for everyone from beginners to intermediate to more advanced bikers. Parking and restrooms are available at 2400 North Walton Blvd, which is just south of Bark Park.

Bella Vista

Bella Vista, a village with a population of 25,250 according to the latest census, covers approximately 65 square miles. It is located on U.S. 71 at the end of I 540 between Bentonville and the Missouri state line. Prior to 2006, when it was incorporated to form a municipality, it was governed by its Property Owners Association (POA). In the beginning, it was first established as an affluent retirement community, but as the years went by, more and more young couples and families moved to the area.

Dining
American
Duffer`s Cafe

Chinese
Top China

Mexican
Verde Limon Mexican
Las Fajitas

Pizza
Gusano`s

Theatre
Sugar Creek 10 Cinema
Sugar Creek Center
Bella Vista, AR
Phone: 479-855-7878

Museums

[Veterans Wall of Honor](#)

The Veterans Wall of Honor, located in Bella Vista, is located in a gorgeous park featuring large native trees, a paved walking trail and a lovely lake, which is home to ducks and geese year round.

The beautiful and unusual circular wall was created to remind all visitors of the enormous sacrifices made by so many to preserve the many freedoms we enjoy today.

Outdoor Recreation

There are seven lakes and eight separate golf courses situated on Bella Vista land that is mostly beautiful wooded rolling hills. Also there are tennis courts, several swimming pools and fitness facilities.

While Bella Vista does have many lakes and golf courses, they are not open to the public at large. **Only property owners and their guests** are allowed to use them, however, if you stay in one of the many rental condos, you can access these facilities as a guest.

Golf – 8 Golf Courses

Some of the most challenging and beautiful golf courses in the state of AR can be found in Bella Vista. There are two executive 9-hole courses and 6 regulation 18-hole courses.

If you need to brush up on your stroke, the Tanyard Creek Practice Center and the Highlands Driving Range are available for those that need to refine their game.

The courses offer multiple sets of tees to suit every golfer's skill level and there are major retail golf shops available at the Kingsdale and Bella Vista Country Club facilities. In Bella Vista, members and their guests can enjoy golf almost year round and at a moderate cost to boot.

Berksdale Golf Course
Kingsdale Golf Shop
4 Kingsdale Lane
Bella Vista, AR 72714
Phone (479) 855-812

Berksdale Golf Course, an 18-hole course, joins with the Kingswood Golf Course to create a 36-hole course called the Kingsdale Golf Complex.

The complex makes use of water, sand, trees and natural terrain to give the golfer, regardless of his or her skill level a challenging round of play. Starting formats vary; check with the golf shop. This popular facility, while the most played, does not have a driving range.

Rental carts and clubs are available in the Kingsdale Golf Shop where you will also find an impressive collection of golfing merchandise.

Branchwood Golf Course
222 Glasgow Road
Bella Vista, AR 72715
(479) 855-8181

This 9-hole par 3 course operates out of the Branchwood Recreation Center. No carts are allowed on this beautiful course carved out of one of the many "hollers" in the area. The entire course off the white tees measures only 1,220 yds, with the longest hole being 153 yds.

Brittany Golf Course
Metfield Golf Shop
1 Euston Drive
Bella Vista, AR 72714
Phone (479) 855-8160

The Brittany executive 9-hole course rounds out the 27-hole Metfield Golf Complex. Five par 3's and four par 4's make this an unusual course. From the No. 3 tees the course plays to 1,696 yds and from the No. 2 tees the course measures 1,889 yds. Both inexperienced and experienced players can be challenged here. Starting formats vary; check with the golf shop.

The Bella Vista Country Club Golf Course
2271 Bella Vista Way
Bella Vista, AR 72714
Phone (479) 855-8003.

This is the oldest golf course in Bella Vista and is classic in design. It gently rolls along U.S. 71 through the valley, but there are few hills so that walking the course is possible. There are four sets of tees so that everyone's skill level can be challenged. Golf carts and rental clubs are available and starting formats vary.

The Dogwood Hills Golf Course
Metfield Golf Shop
1 Euston Drive
Bella Vista, AR 72714
Phone (479) 855-8160

The Dogwood Hills Golf Course joins with the Brittany Golf Course to make up the 27-hole Metfield Golf Complex. Be aware that the course is a links style course, which does not allow you to return to the clubhouse until the 18th green.

The course meanders through woodland, rural area and Metfield's townhouses to provide a terrific and challenging golfing experience. While the terrain is fairly gentle, there are several long stretches from greens to the next tee.

Starting formats vary; check with the clubhouse.

The Highlands Golf Course
1 Pamona Drive
Bella Vista, AR 72715
Phone (479) 855-8150

Consisting of rolling terrain with many, many trees, the Highlands Golf Course opened in 1990. While offering extremely beautiful views, it does present plenty of opportunity for both challenging play and lost balls. There are four sets of tees to accommodate all skill levels and there is a driving range right by the golf shop.

After 2 p.m., a golf cart will be included in the green fee and the driving range is closed on Monday's for maintenance. Starting formats vary; check with the golf shop.

The Kingswood Golf Course
Kingsdale Golf Shop
4 Kingsdale Lane
Bella Vista, AR 72714
Phone (479) 855-8123

The Kingswood Golf Course combines with the Berksdale Golf Course to form the Kingsdale Golf Complex. More than 33% of all the total rounds of golf played in Bella Vista are played at this popular links style course. Note: You do not return to the clubhouse until the 18th green.

Golf carts and rental clubs are available and the largest selection of golfing merchandise in all of Bella Vista can be found at the Kingsdale Golf Shop, however, there is no driving range at this course. Starting formats vary; check with the golf shop.

Scotsdale Golf Course
50 Scotsdale Drive
Bella Vista, AR 72715
Phone (479) 855-8140

This course features a killer back nine with holes 11 through 15 taking you on a roller coaster ride of challenging golf. The front nine moves through gently rolling terrain and offers a fair test of your skills, but is definitely not as demanding as the back nine.

Rental carts and clubs are available and after 2 p.m., a golf cart will be included in the green fee. Starting formats vary; check with the golf shop.

Tanyard Creek Practice Center
10 Nature Trail Lane

Bella Vista, AR 72715
Phone (479) 855-8133

PGA Golf Professional Mike Singletary hosts The Tanyard Creek Practice Center Golf Shop where you will find a huge selection of golfing equipment, which can be individually fitted to suit each golfer and his or her game. The equipment is offered either at or below Internet prices and if you desire to perfect your game, there are three Class "A" PGA Golf Professionals that offer lessons at the center.

There are 28 uncovered and eight covered hard surface stations, which are heated for inclement weather and cold temperatures. Additionally, there are two indoor bays, a launch monitor to assist with club fittings, a practice area with chipping stations and bunkers and a putting green.

Lakes

Lake Rayburn
Size: 47 Acres
Depth: 45 - 50 Ft.
Restrictions: No Wake
Boat Access: North on Hwy 71
Exit onto Kingsland Road heading east. Take the first left, turn onto Lakeside Drive and follow to the lake.

Lake Ann
Size: 112 Acres
Depth: 65 - 70 Ft.
Full Sport Lake,
Water Skiing, tubing, boogie board,
Shoreline Mooring Rental, first come basis
Shoreline Rack Storage for Canoes, Jon Boats

Lake Avalon
Size: 67 Acres
Depth: 40 - 50 Ft.
Restrictions: No Wake

Heated boat dock for winter fishing
Shoreline Mooring Rental, first come basis
Shoreline Rack Storage for Canoes, Jon Boats

Lake Norwood
Size: 35 Acres
Depth: 70 - 75 Ft.
Restrictions: No Wake
Boat Access: East off 340 (Lancashire Blvd) and 71 Hwy, behind Town Center.
Shoreline Rack Storage for Canoes, Jon Boats

Loch Lomond
Size: 475 Acres
Depth: 80 - 85 Ft.
Full Sport Lake,
Water Skiing, Tubing, Boogie Board
Marina docking is available
Motorized Fishing Boats available
for rent by the hour with POA ID card.

Lake Windsor
Size: 220 Acres
Depth: 75 - 80 Ft.
No Restrictions: Full Sport Lake,
Water Skiing, Tubing, Boogie Board
Shoreline Mooring Rental, first come basis

Lake Brittany
Size: 35 Acres
Depth: 70 - 75 Feet
Restrictions: No Wake
Boat Access:

Festivals

Bella Vista Arts & Crafts Festival
1991 Forest Hills Blvd.
Bella Vista, AR

The popular Bella Vista Arts and Crafts Festival is held annually on the third weekend of October. The proceeds from the Bella Vista Arts & Crafts Festival go entirely to support the arts, artists and artisans in Northwest Arkansas.

Eureka Springs

Image credit Arkansas.com

Eureka Springs is a unique Victorian resort village located in NWA in the Ozark Mountains of Carroll County, Arkansas. The village has very steep narrow winding streets lined with delightful Victorian-style cottages and manors. The city, in its entirety, is on the National Register of Historic Places and is a popular tourist attraction in NWA.

The downtown area features an alpine style character, with many old Victorian buildings mostly constructed of local stone. The main streets curve around and up and down the hills making up a five-mile loop. Some of the stores along the main drag have both an upstairs and a downstairs entrance. The National Trust for Historic Preservation has selected Eureka as one of *America's Distinctive Destinations.*

While Eureka hosts a goodly number and variety of events every year, it is also an area where artists, sculptors and poets tend to congregate. There are yearly weekend celebrations for jazz, blues, classical and folk music; and in the summer, full operatic productions with orchestra are presented. Additionally, there is a popular poetry festival held each year and there is, of course, local theatre with numerous productions. Theatre is held downtown at the 1929 large stone auditorium, which was inaugurated with a concert by John Phillip Sousa.

Annual events include four annual *Diversity Weekends* for gays and lesbians, a UFO conference and several different auto shows including one each for Corvettes, Mustangs and Volkswagens.

Many films like Pass the Ammo, Chrystal and Elizabethtown have used Eureka and its surrounding area as their setting. Also, the 1982 mini series "The Blue and the Gray" was filmed in the area, as was the 13th episode of the Ghost Hunters.

Annually, in May, the city plays host to the May Fine Arts Festival. The celebration, which defines Eureka's creativity in the Arts, begins with what is called an Artrageous Parade. Additional events during the month long festival include: A Gallery Stroll where strollers tour the galleries and meet the artists. A PT Cruiser show is on the second Saturday. And there are many other festivals and events including: Books in Bloom, Shakespeare in the Ozarks, White Street Studio Walk and ART Car Festival. Additionally, live music is featured every weekend in Basin Park.

What the Locals Say…

Eureka Springs Has Something For Everyone - Bikers live it up at the Pied Piper Pub and Cathouse Lounge. Christians love the Passion Play. Mountain bikers enjoy Lake Leatherwood. Fishermen and women take joy in the White River, Kings River and Beaver Lake.

Restaurants - K J's Caribe', Local Flavor, Sparky's, Mud Street Restaurants, Café Amore'. NWA favorite Taste of Thai is on the way.

Downtown Shops And Galleries Are Very Cool – Just walk in a few and be pleasantly surprised.

Turpentine Creek Wildlife Refuge Is Great – A great activity for the entire family.

Jim Fains Herbacy Is Excellent – The staff is very knowledgeable and friendly. You'll find natural potions and vitamins.

Last but not least if you would like additional information on Eureka Springs, be sure to check out the site Eureka Springs.org (http://www.eurekasprings.org). They have a wealth of information about different upcoming events.

Arts

83 Spring Street Gallery
83 Spring St.
Eureka Springs, AR 72632
Phone (479) 253-8310

The main Studio Gallery for sculptor Mark Hopkins, 83 Spring Street Gallery has an impressive collection of his artwork including retired and sold-out pieces. The gallery also features: Doug Hall, John Bundy, Don Goin, Kate Barger, Betsy Stafford, Allison Cantrell and other local artists.

OUT on Main Gallery and Pottery
269 N. Main St.
Eureka Springs, AR 72632
Phone (479) 253-8449

Shop for art where the art is actually made. Unique handmade pottery in pitfire, Raku and horse-hair finishes.

Fire Om Earth Retreat Center
8872 Mill Hollow Rd
Eureka Springs, AR 72632
Phone (479) 363-9402

Tai Chi, Belly Dance and Yoga are offered in ongoing classes. Additionally, there are creative workshops, private and group retreats and house concerts.

Quicksilver
73 Spring Street
Eureka Springs, AR 72632
Phone (479) 253-7679

Two shopping levels feature the art of 120 artists. Many are local, but there are also works by regional and nationally known artists. Wall tapestries, wildlife watercolors, photographs, jewelry, pottery and limited edition prints are all on display.

Dining In Eureka Springs
Fine Dining
Autumn Breeze Restaurant
Devito's of Eureka Springs
Gaskins Cabin Steakhouse
The Grand Tavern

Casual Dining
American and International
Local Flavor
Sparky's Roadhouse
Mud Street Cafe
The Garden Bistro
Simply Scrumptious Tea Room
Roadhouse

Asian
Mei Li Cuisine
Lucky Dragon Café (Berryville)

Breakfast
Local Flavor
Mud Street Cafe
New Delhi Cafe

German
Bavarian Inn

Italian
Café Amore'
Ermilio's
Geraldi's Restaurant
Chelsea's Corner Café

Mediterranean
Cottage Inn

Mexican
KJ's Caribe'
Oasis

Romantic
Stonehouse

Day Entertainment
Culinary School-Cuisine Karen
(479) 253-7461

Friday is demonstration and Saturday is hands-on. Take advantage of this French-style cooking class from 10 a.m.- 2 p.m.

Steve's Stables
At Pine Mountain Lodge
1218 Highway 23 S
Eureka Springs, AR 72632
Phone (479) 253-5877

This is a wonderful way and opportunity to spend time with the children. The cost is $25 per person per hour for fun guided trail ride. Rides are limited to not more than 6 riders.

Olden Days Carriage Services
Main St.
Eureka Springs, AR 72632
Phone (479) 981-1737

Experience historical romantic carriage rides. Great for weddings. Kids are always welcome.

Eureka Springs & North Arkansas Railway
299 North Main St.
Eureka Springs, AR 72632
Phone (479) 253-9623

Relive the locomotive transportation history of days gone by enjoying either the Excursion Train or the 1920s Eurekan Dining Car. Let clickety-clack take you back while you enjoy its sumptuous cuisine.

The Palace Bathhouse

135 Spring St.
Eureka Springs, AR 72632
Phone (479) 253-8400

For those that want to be pampered and also have a taste for unique accommodations, you might pay a visit to the Palace Hotel & Bath House. Originally built in 1901, it has been completely restored giving close attention to the original detail. It is listed on the National Historic Register and is really worth visiting.

All suites have the following: TV, wet bar, double size water-jet spa and a king size bed. A delicious continental breakfast is served every morning to each suite.

The only Victorian-era bathhouse that is still in operation is within the Hotel. The bathhouse offers visitors the opportunity to pamper themselves in the calming bliss of a whirlpool bath and massage therapy. Guests soak in original claw foot tubs, or they can take themselves back in time to the turn of the century and indulge themselves with a eucalyptus steam treatment in the very same wooden barrels as travelers of yesteryear used to do.

Staff massage therapists are available for massage treatments. They use the Swedish technique, which emphasizes athletic massage. Typically, guests choose The Works, which consists of whirlpool mineral bath, a revitalizing clay masque, a eucalyptus steam and a massage to top it off.

Eureka Springs School Of The Arts
15751 US 62 W
Eureka Springs, AR 72632
Phone (479) 253-5384

Let noted and award-winning artists and crafts professionals guide you to learn new skills and art forms. Emerging artists can take advantage of regular workshops as they are offered throughout the year.

Hotels In Eureka Springs

Image credit Arkansas.com

1886 Crescent Hotel & Spa
Palace Hotel & Bath House
Quality Inn & Suites
Best Western Inn of the Ozarks
Land O Nod
Eureka Suites
Basin Park Magnuson Grand
Swiss Village Inn

Bed & Breakfast
Harvest House Bed & Breakfast
Red Bud Manor
Main Street Inn
Peabody House Historic Inn
Inn at Rose Hall Bed & Breakfast
Evening Shade Inn B&B
Arsenic and Old Lace

Cottages & Cabins
Cherokee Mountain Log Cabin Resort
Treehouse Cottages
Historic Cottages of Lake Lucerne
Heart of the Hills Inn
Lake Shore Cabins on Beaver Lake
Ozark Rental Cabins
Whispering Hills Cabins
Beaver Lakefront Cabins
Sugar Ridge Resort
Beaver Lake Cottages
Winterwood Lakeside Cottage

Nightlife & Entertainment

Image credit Arkansas.com

The New Great Passion Play
935 Passion Play Road
Eureka Springs, AR 72632
(479) 253-9200

Witness the greatest story ever told in America's #1 attended outdoor drama theatre. The play is held in an outdoor amphitheater and has live animals and hundreds of cast members. Visitors come from all over the world to witness this one-of-a-kind outdoor drama.

Opera in the Ozarks
16311 US 62
W. Eureka Springs, AR 72632
Phone (479) 253-8595

Following a month of study and practice by university students and graduates in Instrumental Music and related arts, three opera performances are put on each summer.

Season schedule and tickets available at our website.

Eureka Live Underground
35 ½ N. Main St.
Eureka Springs, AR 72632
Phone (479) 253-7020

Located in Historic Downtown Eureka, it's a bar with live music and an outdoor beer garden during the warm months. Entrees, appetizers, wine, beer and a full bar are available.

Henri's Just One More
19 ½ Spring Street
Eureka Springs, AR 72632
Phone (479) 253-5797

Friendly and comfortable, Henri's One More features a Martini Bar, appetizers, salads, sandwiches, burgers, specials and a Karaoke deck.

Recreation

Photo compliments of Turpentine Creek

Turpentine Creek Wildlife Refuge
239 Turpentine Creek Lane
Eureka Springs, AR 72632
Phone (479) 253-5841

For a wonderful experience for the entire family visit this shelter for large cats (lions, tigers, etc.). The shelter rescues these distressed animals from anywhere in the USA.

Beaver Bridge
HWY 187
Beaver, AR 72632

Bring your camera and snap away while you visit this famous one-lane bridge. It is called the Little Golden Gate and is well worth the ride from town. On the north side of the river, there is a short hiking trail.

Cosmic Cavern
6386 Hwy. 21 N,
Berryville, AR 72616
Phone (870) 749-2298

Tour through one of the Ozarks' most beautiful caves. View two underground lakes billed as bottomless, one with trout, some of which are blind and colorless from being in the dark some 50 years.

Silent Splendor features one of the longest soda straw formations in the Ozarks and is one of Arkansas' most incredible underground jewels. Go gemstone panning and keep what you find. It's a terrific learning adventure for everyone in the family and its open every day.

Kings River – Riverside Canoe Service
3031 Hwy 62 West
Berryville, AR 72616
Phone (870) 423-3116
Reservations: (800) 528-4645

A float trip for everyone! Half day, full day or weekend float trips covering the entire Kings River are available. Canoe rentals, shuttle service, guide service and canoe sales. You will find one of their float trips designed for you.

Lake Leatherwood City Park
1303 CR 204
Eureka Springs, AR 72632
Phone (479) 253-7921

Open March 1 through mid-November. Sixteen hundred acres of beautiful Ozark Mountain countryside, Lake Leatherwood City Park offers an 85-acre spring-fed lake, hiking, picnicking, walking-trails, mountain biking, camping, cabins and a small marina for boating, canoes and paddleboats. Fun for the entire family

White River –Beaver Dam Store
Hwy. 187
Eureka Springs, AR 72632
Phone (479) 253-6154

Popular and convenient shopping for all your river adventure needs. Bait and tackle, lake maps, fishing instructions, information on fishing guides, fly tying and fly fishing instructions, canoe rentals and rafting on the White River.

Christ of The Ozarks Statue
The New Great Passion Play
935 Passion Play Road
Eureka Springs, AR 72632
(479) 253-9200

Located on the grounds of the New Great Passion Play and free to view is the seven-story high Christ of the Ozarks statue. It was completed in 1966 and was sculpted by Emmet Sullivan, one of the artisans who sculpted Mount Rushmore. The statue's massive arm spread from fingertip to fingertip is 65 feet.

Thorncrown Chapel
12968 Highway 62 W
Eureka Springs, AR 72632
(479) 253-7401

Available for visitation, retreats and weddings daily! Designed by renowned architect E. Fay Jones, Thorncrown Chapel is a stunning 6,000 square foot, 48-foot tall glass structure that has 425 windows. Hidden deep in a wooded setting, the wood and glass creation has been described as the most beautiful chapel in the world.

Open for Sunday worship in the Worship Center from April – October at 9:00 a.m. and 11:00 a.m. Sunday worship in the Chapel from June – October 7:30 a.m., Sunday worship in the Chapel November –December 11:00 a.m. Admission is free, but donations are gratefully accepted.

Shopping

Downtown Eureka Springs

Downtown Eureka Springs is an eclectic collection of stores encompassing everything from art galleries featuring sculpture, paintings, fine jewelry to quaint shops selling local crafts including wood carvings, pottery, weavings or it could be something as unusual as CDs tied to a tree.

There are also a number of great little local restaurants and street vendors where you can get a bite to eat, take a load off your feet and review all the great purchases you've made for the day. Many people from surrounding towns come to Eureka just for the plentiful and one-of-a-kind shopping opportunities.

Fain's Herbacy
61 N. Main St.
Eureka Springs, AR 7263
Phone 479-253-5687

Fain's Herbacy is where the locals go to do their shopping for herbs and vitamins. Founded by Dr. Jim Fain, PhD with the ultimate goal of providing scientifically supported supplements to the community at the lowest prices.

Kaleidokites
1C Spring St.
Eureka Springs, AR 72632
Phone (479) 253-6596

Billing itself as a small store that offers a LARGE selection of kaleidoscopes and kites, Kaleidokites is a store that the kids will love and the parents will enjoy. It is one of the most unusual and adorable shopping experiences in all of NWA.

Two Dumb Dames Fudge Factory

33 S. Main St.
Eureka Springs, AR
Phone (479) 253-7268

They make the fudge right on the premises and it really is the best fudge you can buy anywhere. They also have a full line of "Made in America" toys, games, wind chimes and T-shirts. Gift baskets are available for birthdays, weddings, anniversaries and any old day you can think of and they ship their fudge.

Tummy Ticklers
51 1/2 S Main St
Eureka Springs, AR 72632
Phone (479) 253-6120
Off the sidewalk, across from the Courthouse

Enter, only if you love to eat. Tummy Ticklers Kitchen Store is a wonderful popular little kitchen store filled with unique and useful kitchen gadgets, utensils, fresh coffee beans, jams, Rada Cutlery and loose teas. If you enjoy shopping different kitchen stores, you'll love this tiny little store.

Fayetteville

Image Credit Arkansas.com

Fayetteville, with a population of 73,570 according to the latest 2010 Census, is located on the edge of the Boston Mountains deep within the Ozark Mountains. The pride and joy of the city is the University of Arkansas. Fayetteville is the flagship campus for the University of Arkansas.

During the fall and spring, thousand of students come to the city to attend the university, which greatly changes the complexion of this NWA city. Additionally, during the school term when the University of Arkansas Razorbacks are active, thousands of fans throng to Fayetteville to support the various sports programs participated in by the University. The Razorbacks are top contenders in the SEC conference and are supported by thousands of enthusiastic fans.

While baseball, basketball and football are typically in the limelight, the University of Arkansas is also very proud of its track and field program, which has won 42 national championships to date.

Forbes ranked Fayetteville 7th best college sports town and 8th best for Business and Careers. U.S. News ranked Fayetteville one of the best places to retire. Close to Bentonville, the home of Wal-Mart, the city plays host in the Bud Walton Arena to the thousands of Wal-Mart shareholders at their annual meeting. Additionally, Forbes named the Fayetteville-Springdale-Rogers area as the second-best area in the U.S. for recovery from the current U.S. recession.

What the Locals Say…

Musts To Do And See In Fayetteville - Dickson Street Bookshop, Dickson Street, Downtown Fayetteville Square and the University of Arkansas.

Favorite Restaurants - Pesto Café, Greenhouse Grill, Buck Nekkid BBQ, 1936 Café, El Camino Real, Cable Car Pizza, Catfish Hole,

Bikes, Blues and BBQ - Approximately 400,000 people attend the yearly Bikes, Blues and BBQ held in September of each year. This popular event includes free music, a huge BBQ contest and numerous motorcycle events. It is wild and wildly popular.

Ozark Mountains Hiking, Biking And Camping – The picturesque Ozark Mountains are the perfect place to enjoy fun outdoor activities like hiking, biking and camping.

Buffalo River - Canoeing on the popular nearby Buffalo River is always fun.

Calling The Hogs - If you are in town for one of the University of Arkansas' famous Razorback basketball or football, don't miss the faithful fans calling the hogs. It is really an experience you won't forget.

Last but not least if you would like additional information on Fayetteville, be sure to check out the website Experience Fayetteville (http://www.experiencefayetteville.com/). They have a wealth of information about different upcoming events.

Arts

Image credit Arkansas.com

Walton Arts Center
495 W. Dickson St.
Fayetteville, AR 72701
Phone (479) 443-5600

Located in the heart of Dickson Street, Walton Arts Center is the largest venue for the performing arts and entertainment in NWA. More than 150,000 people annually are drawn to numerous Broadway musicals, dance performances, comedy shows and theater productions at the Walton Arts Center.

Fayetteville Underground Art
(Opening September 2012)
101 West Mountain,
Fayetteville, AR

Fayetteville Underground is a studio/gallery space in downtown Fayetteville. They offer studios to working artists as well as the opportunity to be selected as an artist member (without studio space). They host shows by residents as well as visiting artists.

Arts Live Theatre
818 North Sang Avenue
Fayetteville, AR
(479) 521-4932

Arts Live Theatre, through summer youth theater training programs offers after-school theatre programs, MainStage production and a Youthfest production.

Symphony of Northwest Arkansas
P.O. Box 1243
Fayetteville, AR 72702

The Symphony of Northwest Arkansas (SoNA) is an outstanding 70-piece orchestra and has, for more than 50 years, entertained and educated NWA audiences. (SoNA), in partnership with Walton Art Center, desires to lead their audiences in an exploration of universal truths and beauty. Thus enabling them to connect, stimulate and enrich Arkansas, particularly the Northwest region, through musical performances of uncompromising quality.

Terra Studios
12103 County Road 47
Fayetteville, AR 72701
Phone (479) 643-3185

Watch skilled glassworkers create the now famous Bluebird of Happiness. Artisans also produce glass and pottery gifts, house wares and fine art pieces. Terra Studios is located in the Ozark Mountains near Fayetteville where visitors can stroll along the wooded paths and through the mural garden and explore the pottery showroom.

A Pottery Studio
2002 S. School

Fayetteville, AR 72701
Phone (479) 521-3171

Classes and workshops conducted by some of the world's top artists and potters and covering all areas of ceramics and pottery are offered. Enjoy and explore one of the oldest crafts in existence.

Heartwood Gallery
428 S. Government Street
Fayetteville, AR 72701
Phone (479) 444-0888

Matt Miller Studio
21 West Mountain St., Suite 26
On The Square
Fayetteville, AR 72701
Phone (870) 919-8651

Dining In Fayetteville

Fine Dining
1936 Cafe & Club
Bordinos
Ella's Restaurant
Theo's

Casual Dining
American Food
Greenhouse Grille
Hugo's
AQ Chicken House
Mama Dean's Soul Food
Catfish Hole
Feltner Brothers

Asian
Hu Hot Mongolian Grill
Pho Quyen
Twin Kitchen
Meiji Japanese Cuisine
Thep Thai Restaurant
A Taste of Thai
Sala Thai
Pho Saigon
Hunan's Manor Chinese Restaurant

Bakery
Rick's Bakery

BBQ
Lucky Luke's BBQ
Sassy's Red House
Boar's Nest BBQ
Whole Hog Cafe
Wes's Bar-B-Que

The Bar-B-Q Place
Buck Nekkid BBQ
Penguin Ed's
Herman's Rib House

Breakfast
Common Grounds
Village Inn
Razors Edge
Ozark Lanes
Greenhouse Grille (Sunday Brunch)
Cafe Rue Orleans (Sunday Brunch)
Emelia's Kitchen (Sunday Brunch)

Cajun
Cafe Rue Orleans
Lyn D.'s Cajun Gypsy

Coffee Houses
Jammin Java
Big Momma's Coffee & Espresso Bar
Mama Carmen's Global Cafe
Silver Joe's Coffee
Common Grounds

European
Teatro Scarpino

Greek
Kosmos Greekafe

Italian
Pesto Cafe
Fresco Cafe & Pub
Geraldi's
Noodles Italian Kitchen
Spiedini Italian Grill
Vetro 1925

Mediterranean
Emelia's Kitchen
Petra Cafe

Mexican
Mojitos
Celi's True Mexican Cuisine
Chipotle Mexican Grill
La Huerta
Qdoba Mexican Grill
Burrito Loco

Sandwich Shops
Hammontree's Gourmet
Little Bread Company
Loafin' Joe's
The Green Submarine Espresso Cafe and Sub Shop
Atlanta Bread Co.

Pizza
Cable Car Pizza
Damgoode Pies
Gusano's Chicago-Style Pizzeria
Mellow Mushroom
Mojo's Pints and Pies
Tim's Pizza
U.S. Pizza Co.
Bariola's Pizza
Geno's Pizza
Jim's Razorback Pizza
Mordours Pizza
Tiny Tim's/West Mt. Brewing co
Ye Olde King Pizza
Geraldi's

Seafood
Catfish Hole
Mermaids

Powerhouse Seafood & Grill
Red Lobster

Festivals

County Fairs

Benton and Washington County Fairs are held from mid to late August every year. The Fairs are a true fall tradition and are enjoyed for their livestock shows, fair foods, special events and rides.

Lights of the Ozarks

The spirit of the holidays comes alive each year as millions of lights cover the Fayetteville town square. Families and visitors alike flock to the area to enjoy celebration of the holiday spectacle beginning the day before Thanksgiving through New Year's Day.

Hotels In Fayetteville

Luxury Accommodations
Homewood Fayetteville
Staybridge Suites
TownePlace Suites

Mid-Range Accommodations
Candlewood Suites
Holiday Inn Express
Comfort Inn & Suites
Hampton Inn
Clarion Hotel
Quality Inn
Travelodge Inn & Suites

B&B
Dickson Street Inn
Pratt Place Inn & Barn

Museums

Arkansas Air Museum
4290 S. School
Next to Drake Field
Fayetteville, AR 72701
(479) 521-4947

Select either a self-guided tour or arrange for a guide. The museum has a wonderful collection of aircraft from the 1920s – 1940s and is a terrific opportunity to relive the barnstorming days of early aviation. Imagine seeing a World War I fighter plane, next to the sleek "Mystery Ship", winner of the 1929 National Air Race and star of two movies. The Arkansas Air Museum is great for families and a fun and educational way to spend a couple of hours.

Arkansas Country Doctor Museum
109 N. Starr Ave.
Lincoln, AR 72744
Phone (479) 824-4307

See a diverse collection of medical equipment including medical instruments, an iron lung and a dental chair and equipment from the 1930s. The museum was founded in 1994 by Dr. Harold Boyer to honor the heroic achievements and selfless service of Arkansas country doctors. The museum was used as a clinic and private home by three different Arkansas Doctors who lived and worked on the premises from 1936 -1973. Open Wed-Sat 1:00pm- 4:00pm Admission is free.

Clinton House Museum
930 West Clinton Drive
Fayetteville, AR 72701
Phone (479) 444-0066

The museum was the wedding site and first home of Bill and Hillary Clinton. The museum is a 1930's English-style bungalow, which showcases the life and times of the Clintons during their years in Fayetteville. The museum has a gift shop and features photographic and memorabilia displays, including vintage campaign materials. It is available for public tours, small meetings, receptions and weddings. .

Confederate Cemetery - Fayetteville, Arkansas
500 E. Rock
Rock & Willow Streets
Fayetteville, AR
Phone (479) 521-1710

Overlooking Fayetteville, this beautiful old cemetery is situated on 3 acres and was established in 1872 by a group of women who founded the Southern Memorial Association. The remains of some 500 Confederate soldiers from Texas, Missouri, Louisiana and Arkansas rest here. Many of the soldiers fell during the battles of Pea Ridge and Prairie Grove. The cemetery is on the Register of Historic Places and welcomes visitors from dawn until dusk.

Evergreen Cemetery
University and Williams Street
Fayetteville, AR

Listed on the National Register of Historical Places, Evergreen Cemetery has over 3000 interments and is the final resting place for many Confederate Soldiers. It is the burial site of Arkansas soldier, statesman and Governor Archibald Yell as well as Senator J. William Fulbright, the educator Sophia Sawyer and the industrialist Lafayette Gregg.

Fayetteville National Cemetery
700 S. Government
Fayetteville, AR 72701
Phone (479) 444-5051

The cemetery is the burial site for 1,600 Union soldiers along with hundreds of other veterans who have lost their lives since. Fayetteville National Cemetery is one of the oldest military cemeteries in the South.

Headquarters House
118 E. Dickson St.
Fayetteville, AR 72701
Phone (479) 521-2970

During the Civil War, this home was the headquarters for both the Confederate and Union armies. It was originally built by Judge Jonas Tebbets in 1853. Today, it is the headquarters for the Washington County Historical Society. To arrange a tour of the home, call the above number.

Ozark Military Museum
4360 S. School Ave.
Fayetteville, AR 72701
Phone (479) 587-1941

Located at the Fayetteville Airport, the museum has a varied collection of military related equipment including: 15 military vehicles including three models of the familiar Willys Jeep, WWII WC-54 Ambulance, Korean M37 3/4-ton cargo truck, 2 1/2-ton 6x6 cargo truck used in Desert Storm and a British Ferret light armored scout car, a WWII Aeronca L-3 observation aircraft and a Beech 3NM (Twin Beech) known as the "CANADIAN QUEEN" which served in the Royal Canadian Air Force from 1952 to 1967.

Additionally, the museum also has 12 static and restoration project aircraft including a UH-1 Huey, A-7 Corsair II, T-2 Buckeye, T-33, SNJ, NE-1, L-13 restoration and a JRB restoration.

Some other interesting artifacts on display include a Civil War tent stove, gas mask, items from the Home front WWII, WWII German daggers, WWII helmets and unit patches.

Prairie Grove Battlefield State Park
Prairie Grove, AR
(479) 846-2990

Nationally recognized Prairie Grove Battlefield State park is one of America's most intact Civil War battlefields. Visitors can drive the 6 1/2 mile tour or take the 1-mile Battlefield trail, which features wayside exhibits.

Fayetteville Public Library
401 W. Mountain St.
Fayetteville, AR 72702
Phone (479) 571-2222

The library is a beautiful 88,000 square foot building, which houses a comprehensive genealogical collection, the Fulbright Fireplace Room and it has extensive programming for children and adults. It was chosen in 2005 as the destination library for the Thomson Gale/Library Journal Library of the Year award.

The library's many services include: local newspaper, free internet access for visitors, popular magazines, music, movie and audio books, fiction and non-fiction materials and online databases. The Fayetteville Public Library has a cafe on site.

Nightlife/Entertainment

Dickson Street
Downtown
Fayetteville, AR 72701

People of all ages enjoy Dickson Street. It is the place to see and be seen in Fayetteville. The streets are filled with unusual and colorful shops, galleries, restaurants and clubs and the atmosphere is typically quite lively. The college crowd loves Dickson Street as it is located close to the University of Arkansas, but people from all over NWA frequent the area for its music, terrific shops and unique restaurants.

George's Majestic Lounge
519 W. Dickson
Fayetteville, AR 72701
Phone (479) 527-6618

Patio and Live Music

Arkansas Music Pavilion
2536 N McConnell Ave
Fayetteville, AR, 72704
Phone (479) 443-5600

Some of the world's top performers appear at "the AMP". It is a stunning fully covered open-air pavilion, which is the venue for outdoor arts and summer entertainment.

Theatres

112 Drive In
3352 Hwy 112 N.
Fayetteville, AR 72707
Phone (479) 442-4542

Yes, it's a real outdoor drive in movie that features recent full-length movies. A real movie going adventure, the 112 Drive In is one of the very few left in the entire country. .

Razorback Theatre
3956 N. Steele Ave
Fayetteville, AR 72703
Phone (479) 442-4542

Stadium seating movie theater with 16 screens showing current movies located near restaurants and shopping.

Regal Fiesta Square 16
3033 N. College Ave
Fayetteville, AR 72703
Phone (479) 575-0393

16 screen theater showing current movies.

Shopping

Downtown Square

Fayetteville's downtown square is a wonderful place to visit. It is home to many restaurants, unusual shops, historic buildings and modern offices and is often the focal point for many local activities. You will be delighted by the well-tended square gardens with their dazzling array of colorful flowers.

Bath Junkie

641 West Dickson Street
Fayetteville, Arkansas 72701
479-444-0211

Mix and match your favorite scents and colors into luxurious lotions, bubble baths, bath salts, etc. Bath Junkie is truly a delightful experience for the senses.

Dickson Street Bookshop

325 W. Dickson Street
Fayetteville, AR 72701
Phone (479) 442-8182

Those who love books will need to prepare themselves for a real treat! You can easily lose a few hours in this funky shop filled with treasured books.

Used and out of print books
Hours: Mon-Sat 9-9 Sun 11-6

Fayetteville Farmers Market

Downtown Fayetteville Square
Phone (479) 236- 2910

Fayetteville's downtown square is the place to go on Tuesday, Thursday and Saturday mornings from April –

October. Select from the best of locally grown produce, plants, flowers, honey and native crafts. Meet the growers and the artisans in person and have some hot coffee and donuts from vendors on the square and nearby restaurants.

Nightbird Books
205 W Dickson Street
Fayetteville, Ar
(479) 443 - 2080

Nightbird Books is a locally owned, independent bookstore featuring a wide variety of hand-selected new books for adults and children.

Northwest Arkansas Mall
4201 N. Shiloh Dr.
Fayetteville, AR 72703
Phone (479) 521-6151

Fayetteville's Northwest Arkansas Mall has a huge variety of specialty shops, national stores and dining venues. It is the largest shopping facility in NWA and there is always plenty going on at the Fayetteville's Mall.

Sports & Recreation In Fayetteville

Image credit Arkansas.com

Donald Reynolds Razorback Stadium
Razorback Road
University of Arkansas Campus
Fayetteville, AR 72701
Phone (479) 57505255

The University of Arkansas' football stadium was renovated in 2001, has a seating capacity of 80,000 and features a 30' high by 107' wide LED video display. The display brings amazing graphics and replay to virtually every fan in the stadium.

Bud Walton Arena
Razorback Rd. & Leroy
University of Arkansas Campus

Fayetteville, AR 72701 Phone
(479) 575-8618

There is no place in the U.S. that can match the roaring atmosphere of Bud Walton Arena. Because there are more seats in less space than any other facility in the world, the yelling and stomping of the fans can be earsplitting. The noise level can be so high that the specially designed spring mounted floor actually shakes.

From the Tommy Boyer Museum and concourse displays, to the sound system and laser light show, to its floor-side seating and mid-level luxury boxes, there is no sports facility that can match its total package.

Baum Stadium
15th Street & Razorback Road
Fayetteville, AR 72701
Phone (479) 575-3655

Baseball America named Baum Stadium the country's No. 1 college baseball facility in 1998. Baseball America's survey stated that the stadium features amenities that put it "in a class of its own." The state-of-the-art 3,300-seat stadium stands as a tribute to the University of Arkansas' baseball program.

Randal Tyson Indoor Track Center
1380 S Beechwood
Fayetteville, AR 72701
Phone (479) 575-5151

One of the finest sports arenas in the U.S. and consistently the host to such track championships as the NCAA National Indoor Championships, SEC Championships and the Tyson Invitational.

Golf

Fayetteville Country Club
The Fayetteville golf course at the Fayetteville Country Club opened in 1919. It is an 18-hole course featuring 6,208 yards of golf from the longest tees, has a slope rating of 132 on Bermuda grass and a course rating of 69.6.

Stonebridge Meadows Golf Course
3495 East Goff Farm Road
Fayetteville, AR 72701
(479) 571-3673

Stonebridge Meadows Golf Course is a beautiful 18-hole public course that is open year round. A golf pro is on site and there is a driving range. Metal spikes are not allowed.

Hiking, Biking & Camping

Image Credit Arkansas.com

Fayetteville City Trails
Fayetteville City Trails features over 18 paved miles of trails. Trails include; Clabber Creek Trail, Dale Clark Park Trail,

Dickson Street/U of A Loop, Fayetteville High School Track, Finger Park, Frisco Trail, Gordon Long Park, Gregory Park Trail, Gulley Park Trail, Joe Clark Trail at Lake Wilson, King Fisher Trail at Lake Sequoyah, Lake Fayetteville Trail, Mount Sequoyah/Historic District Trail, Mud Creek Trail, Scull Creek Trail, Shiloh Trail, St. Paul Trail,
Town Branch Creek Trail, TSA LA GI Trail, Walker Park and Wilson Park Trail.

Buffalo River and Surrounding Area
There are numerous mountain bike trails and camping areas on the outskirts of Fayetteville. Canoeing the Buffalo River is always a favorite.

Botanical Garden of the Ozarks
4703 Crossover Road
Fayetteville, AR 72764
(479) 750-2620

Here, the spirit of the Ozarks is celebrated using a series of expertly designed and intensively maintained outdoor areas. Botanical Garden of the Ozarks also features the unique timber-framed Totemeier Horticulture Center.

Lake Wedington Recreation Area
15592 Lake Wedington Entry Road
Wedington Township, AR 72704
(479) 442-3527

Picnic areas, cabins, camping, hiking, fishing, boating and swimming are available at this scenic 102-acre little forest lake. The total recreation area covers some 424 acres and is an outdoor oasis located only 15 miles west of Fayetteville.

Lake Fayetteville
511 E Lakeview Dr
Fayetteville, AR 72764
Phone (479) 444-3471

Lake Fayetteville is a 194-acre lake on the northern edge of Fayetteville. The park itself is 640 acres and offers many recreational opportunities including: Hiking, picnicking, softball and other sports as well as boating and fishing.

Devil's Den State Park

Outdoor enthusiasts get to explore wild backcountry in Devil's Den State Park and the surrounding Ozark National Forest. The area provides hiking, backpacking and mountain bike trails

Mt. Sequoyah
Mount Sequoyah Retreat & Conference Center
150 NW Skyline Drive
Fayetteville, AR 72701
Phone (479) 760-8126

Mt. Sequoyah is of interesting historical importance as it is part of the Trail of Tears route taken by the Indians on their way to reservations in the West. Named for the Cherokee leader who created the Cherokee alphabet and translated the New Testament into Cherokee. It is the highest point in Fayetteville with an elevation of 1700 ft.

Pig Trail Scenic Drive
The Pig Trail is the most beautiful and scenic route in NWA. Be prepared for plenty of curves. Take Hwy. 16 East out of Fayetteville, turn south on Hwy. 23 to Ozark. To return to Fayetteville, go west on I-40 to Alma, then north on Hwy. 71 or continue west to Fort Smith and go north on Highway 540. Approximately 110 miles round-trip.

Scenic Highway 71/U.S. Highway 540
A scenic loop drive that offers breathtaking vistas of the hills and valleys of the Arkansas Ozarks. Take U.S. 540 in Fayetteville to Scenic Highway 71 and then travel south to I-40. Go west on I-40 to 540 North, which will return you to

Fayetteville.

Lowell

Lowell is a small town in Benton County, Arkansas. According to the 2000 Census the population was 7,327. Lowell is part of the NWA metropolitan area and is headquarters to J. B. Hunt Transport Services, Inc., the country's largest publicly traded transportation company.

Dining

Asian
Palm Noodle

American
Ron's Hamburgers & Chili
Antrim's Pancake House

Pizza
Jim's Razorback Pizza

Outdoor Recreation

Golf Mountain
115 Dixieland Road
Lowell, AR 72745
Phone: (479) 659-0001

NWA's premier mini golf course with 36 holes and many dips, bumps, inclines, water hazards and advanced mini golf multi-textured services.

Rogers

Rogers is located in one of the fastest growing areas in the country. With a population of 55,964 according to the 2010 Census, the Rogers metropolitan area is ranked 109th in terms of populations in the United States.

Rogers is a booming lively community with a terrific shopping district featuring both independent and national stores. The Promenade shopping area along with Village on the Creeks takes a back seat to nobody. Simply stated, if you want something, this shopping mecca will have it.

Rogers is also home to Pinnacle Country Club, a world-class venue for championship golf. Rogers has locally owned as well as multiple chain restaurants that offer delicious fares of all kinds and many are located along the I-540 corridor. The locals call it restaurant row.

What the Locals Say…

Must Things To See And Do When Visiting Rogers – World class shopping and restaurants, Beaver Lake, Hobbs State Park and of course the Historical Downtown Rogers.

Downtown Rogers – The historic district of Rogers offers something for everyone. Everything from shops to restaurants that are available daily, as well as the weekly and monthly events. The weekly events include Pickin' in the park and the fun Farmers Market. The third Friday of each month offers the Twilight Walk. Annual events in downtown Rogers include the Frisco Festival, the Goblin Parade, Christmas in the District and Main Street Rogers Golf Tournament.

Our Favorite Wonderful Restaurants - Bonefish, Catfish John's, Carrabba's, Wesner's, Crabby's, Basil's, Iron Horse and Mister B's to name just a few.

Shop The Promenade – Many terrific shops and upper class national stores to choose from.

5 World Gyms In The Area – Keep fit while you are here. Gyms feature pools, tennis, spin classes, TRX classes, RIPPED, Zumba, Tanning and traditional workout equipment as well. In addition, kids fit classes and childcare are provided

Golfing At Pinnacle Country Club – Pinnacle Country Club in Rogers, Arkansas, offers a remarkable private club experience combining upscale golf, tennis, swim and clubhouse amenities.

Last but not least if you would like additional information on Rogers, be sure to check out the website Visit Rogers (http://www.visitrogersarkansas.com/). They have a wealth of information about different events.

Arts

Rogers Little Theater
116 South 2nd Street
Rogers, AR 72756
(479) 631-8988

Throughout the year in the beautifully restored Victory Theater, The Rogers Little Theater located in historic downtown Rogers presents a variety of dinner theater and also regular performances.

White River Gallery
115 S Second St
Rogers, AR 72756
Phone: (479) 936-5851

Features Ed Cooley art.

Poor Richard's Art
101 West Walnut
Rogers, Arkansas 72756
(479) 636-0417

Poor Richard's Art offers original art and fine craft in a variety of media created from local artists in and around Northwest Arkansas.

Dining In Rogers

Fine Dining
Mister B's
Bonefish Grill
Ruth's Chris Rogers
Crabby's Seafood

Casual Dining
American
Texas Land & Cattle Steak House
Chili's Restaurant
Applebee's
Dixie Cafe
Mimi's Cafe
Outback Steakhouse
Colton's Steak House & Grill
JJ's Grill of Rogers

Asian
PF Chang's China Bistro
Panda

BBQ
Famous Dave's Bar-B-Que
Rib Crib

Breakfast
The Bean Palace
Wesner's Grill (Breakfast is Legendary)
Mimi's Cafe
Log Cabin Family Restaurant
Sam's Olde Tyme Burger
Lucy's Diner

Burgers
Back Yard Burgers

[Five Guys Burgers and Fries](#)
[Red Robin Gourmet Burgers](#)
[Sam's Olde Tyme Burger](#)

Cajun
[Copelands of New Orleans](#)

Coffee Shops
[Iron Horse](#)
[Starbucks](#)
[Silver Joes](#)

Down-home Cooking
[Wesner's Grill](#) (Breakfast is Legendary)
[Susie Q Malt Shop](#)
[Monte Ne Inn Chicken Restaurant](#)

Fish
[Catfish John's](#)
[Fish City Grill](#)

Indian
[Chutney](#)

Italian
[Carrabba's Italian Grill](#)
[Johnny Carinos](#)
[Basils' Cafe](#)

Mexican
[Abuelos](#)
[On the Border Mexican Grill & Cantina](#)
[Rolando's](#)
[Las Palmas](#)
[Maria's Mexican Restaurant](#)

Pizza

Mellow Mushroom Pizza Bakers
The Rail a Pizza Company
Bariola's Pizzeria

Sandwich Shops
Iron Horse
Green Bean
Atlanta Bread Company
Baker Bros American Deli
Crumpet Tea Room
Slim Chickens

Festivals

Frisco Festival
Rogers Downtown Historic District

Billed as the Rogers premiere family fun event, the Frisco Festival is a two-day event that offers live music and other entertainment, contests, vendors and every kind of food imaginable.

Arts & Crafts Events
Festivals and Arts and Crafts are a big deal in NWA. The various events are held in May and October annually and attract more than 250,000 crafts enthusiasts from all over the country. Festivals include: Long's Old Orchard & Farm Arts & Crafts Festival, Ole Applegate Place Autumn Arts & Crafts Festival, Ozark Regional Arts &Crafts Show, Rogers Antique Show & Sale, Rogers Expo Center, Sharp's Show of War Eagle, Spanker Creek Farm Arts & Crafts, War Eagle Fair, War Eagle Mill Antique & Crafts Show, Bella Vista Arts & Crafts, Craft Fair Around the Square, Frisco Station Mall Arts & Crafts, Hillbilly Corner and the Jones Center Arts & Crafts.

Hotels In Rogers
Luxury Accommodations
Embassy Suites Rogers Ar
Country Inn and Suites Rogers Ar
Homewood Suites Rogers AR
Aloft Hotel Rogers Ar
Candlewood Suites
Fairfield Inn & Suites
Hyatt Place
Hilton Garden Inn
Residence Inn by Marriott
Staybridge Suites
TownePlace Suites by Marriott

Mid-Range Accommodations
Hampton Inn
Holiday Inn & Suites

Extended Stay Accommodations
Microtel Inn & Suites
Mainstay Suites

Museums

Image credit Arkansas.com

Pea Ridge National Military Park
Hwy 62 North
Pea Ridge, AR 72751

The Park is located northeast of Rogers and is situated on 4,300 acres. The Pea Ridge Civil War battle honors some 26,000 soldiers who saw action there on March 7-8, 1862. It was fought to secure the upper reaches of the Mississippi and Missouri rivers and to keep the state of Missouri under federal control.

At the park visitors center there is a video, a museum and a gift shop. There is also a self-guided auto tour that features markers and audio descriptions of the battlefield. Additionally, there is a horse and hiking trail.

Rogers Daisy Airgun Museum
202 West Walnut Street

Rogers, AR 72756
Phone (479) 986-6873

The Rogers Daisy Airgun Museum is home to the Daisy Air Rifle and The Daisy BB Gun. People of all ages enjoy this amazing collection. Older visitors can enjoy Daisy models they used when they were young and youths get to see the latest in fascinating air guns, ammo and accessories.

The gift shop has limited edition items that can only be purchased from the museum gift shop.

Tuesday-Saturday 10:00 a.m. – 5:00 p.m.

Rogers Historical Museum
322 South 2nd Street
Rogers, AR 72756
(479) 621-1154

A great way to experience local history through permanent and changing exhibits, educational programs and special events. Fun for the entire family including:

The Attic - Experience the past in a museum within the museum, designed for hands-on fun for all ages.

The 1895 Hawkins House - Step into the early 1900s with a guided tour.

First Street - A fun filled re-creation of a downtown of yesteryear. Youngsters will especially enjoy the "please touch" shelf.

Free admission - Open Tues-Sat 10:00 a.m. - 4:00 p.m. Closed on major holidays.

Outdoor Recreation

Lakes

Image credit Arkansas.com

Beaver Lake
2260 North 2nd Street
Rogers, AR 72756
Phone: (479) 636-1210

Beaver Lake with 487 miles of shoreline is located high in the Ozark Mountains. Completed in 1966 by the U. S. Corps of Engineers, the 28,370-acre lake offers many recreational opportunities including 2008 acres of campgrounds and 650 individual campsites.

Cabins, resorts, marinas, outfitters and spectacular fishing opportunities surround the lake. Other facilities that are available include: Swimming beaches, hiking trails, sanitary dump stations, group picnic shelters and amphitheaters are also available in many of the parks around the lake.

Small mouth bass, largemouth bass and striper bass fishing is excellent on the lake, but there are also ample opportunities to catch bream, crappie, channel and spoonbill catfish and white bass. Beaver Lake is a fisherman's paradise.

FLW Bass Tournament
Prairie Creek Park
9300 North Park Road
Rogers AR 72756
Phone: 479.636.1210

Every year in the spring, the FLW Tour® stops at Rogers and Beaver lake for the Wal-Mart FLW Bass Tournament. The tournament is the Tour's only annual stop and it attracts the media, hundreds of anglers both professional and amateur and their families and friends to the area

Golf

Pinnacle Country Club
The Pinnacle Country Club plays host to the LPGA® Northwest Arkansas Championship, this stunning 530 acre private golf course promises to take its place among the nation's best. This gorgeous course offers golfers of all abilities an enjoyable experience.

Parks

War Eagle Mill
1045 War Eagle Road
Rogers, AR 72756
(479) 789-5343

See an authentic working undershot water-powered gristmill that is still producing all natural organic grains, flours and mixes right before your eyes. American families that live in the Arkansas Ozarks hand-pack the grains.

Eat in the Bean Palace Restaurant or shop in old-fashioned mercantile for unique hand crafted items and packed grains.

Hobbs State Park-Conservation Area
(479)-789-2380

Hobbs State Park is the largest in land area of the 51 state parks in Arkansas. Hobbs State Park is still in its initial development phase at this time. It currently offers many wonderful recreation opportunities for the people of Arkansas including, The Historic Van Winkle Trail, the Pigeon Roost Trail and the Shaddox Hollow Trail. The last two trails are 1.5 mile environmental education loops that explore a variety of Ozark microclimates. In addition, the Park also offers interpretive programs, undeveloped access to Beaver Lake, regulated season hunting and an all-weather public firing range.

Wild Wilderness Drive-Through Safari
20923 Safari Rd
Gentry, AR 72734
Phone (479) 736-8383

Bring your family and spend a wonderful afternoon or an entire day on a 4-mile drive-through seeing wild and exotic animals along the way. The Wilderness drive-through safari is in Gentry, AR and is situated on 400 beautiful acres and it also has several ponds.

Within the park, there are walk-through areas and petting parks for easy and safe interaction with the animals. You may be lucky enough to pet a tiger cub or a snake the day you are there. Every member of your family will enjoy seeing, petting and learning about the animals.

Bring a picnic lunch or enjoy the snack bar. Open everyday at 9:00 a.m. including holidays.

Skydive Skyranch
Hangar 4

Cecil Smith Field
Siloam Springs, AR 72761
Phone: (479) 651-6160

Learn to skydive from committed, experienced staff. Skydive Skyranch provides top-notch jumper support as well as sport parachuting fun. Skyranch can take you from your first jump all the way to the national championship.

War Eagle Cavern On Beaver Lake
Hwy. 12
War Eagle, AR 72756
Phone (479) 789-2909

See fossils, waterfalls, soda straws and domes as you walk through a stunning natural entrance straight into the mountainside. Hear strange and fascinating stories of Draft Dodgers, Outlaws, Indians and Moonshiners. See a bat up close and personal, visit the gift shop and eat at the mouth-watering Smoke Signal Cafe. Or pan for treasure at the War Eagle Mining Company or lose yourself in the Lost in the Woods Maze. Fun for the entire family and really an attraction you don't want to miss.

Fast Lane Entertainment
1117 N. Dixieland St.
Rogers, AR
Phone (479) 659-0999

Fun for the entire family. Voted Best Birthday Party Destination in Northwest Arkansas. Open 365 Days A Year.

Shopping

Image Credit Arkansas.com

Pinnacle Hills Promenade
2203 Promenade Boulevard
Suite 3200
Rogers, AR 72758
(479) 936-2160

The Pinnacle Hills Promenade is considered by many to be the best shopping experience in all of NWA. Dillard's and J.C. Penney are the anchor stores, but there are plenty of other top-quality specialty stores to choose from too. Hungry? The Promenade experience also includes several premium restaurants. Looking for entertainment? Check out the Malco 12-screen theatre.

Historic Downtown Rogers
Rogers, AR

Historic Downtown Rogers is a wonderful blend of sounds, aromas, tastes, sights, textures, cultures and generations where there is always something for every member of the family to do and enjoy. It's a lively community of thriving businesses, eateries, shopping opportunities, art, music, history, theater and professional services.

Scottsdale Center
46th Street
Rogers, AR

Several traditional stores like the Gap, Barnes and Noble and Kohl's occupy the Scottsdale Center located facing I-540 in Rogers. There are also numerous dining options in the Scottsdale Center.

Restaurants such as Copeland's of New Orleans, Carino's, Applebee's, On the Border, Chili's, Famous Dave's, as well as several others also occupy the Center and for entertainment, there is the Rogers Towne Cinema, a 12-screen movie theatre.

Village on the Creeks
Rogers' Pinnacle Hills
Exit 83 off I-540
Rogers, AR

Enjoy a lakeside picnic, visit unique shops, or eat a patio meal. Village on the Creeks is the perfect place to kick back, relax and let the challenges of the day fade away amid their beautifully landscaped public areas, which include streams, gardens, sculptures and fountains.

AG Russell Knives
2900 S. 26th St.
Rogers, AR 72758-8571
Phone (479) 631-0130

This is the granddaddy of all knife stores. Established in 1964 by A.G. Russell, an Arkansas native. You'll see every kind of knife you might think of in the store and they all come with a concrete guarantee. "We guarantee total satisfaction. You, the customer, decides what satisfaction is. You decide how long you are entitled to be satisfied." Guarantees don't get much better than that!

Regular Store Hours: Monday - Friday: 8:30 - 5:00
Saturday: 9:00 - 3:00

Farmers Market
Located in Historic Downtown Rogers
At the corner of Arkansas and Elm
Rogers, AR

Rogers Farmers Market is a seasonal open-air market that offers fresh produce and local crafts. A fun way to spend the morning!

Open May - October

Frisco Station Mall
100 N. Dixieland Road
Rogers, AR 72756
(479) 631-0006

Hobby Lobby anchors this one-level mall, which is also home to 25 additional unusual stores and eating establishments. Frisco Station Mall is a 242,535 square foot, shopping center and since it is all on one level, it attracts many walkers to take advantage of the controlled temperature and the flat surface.

Springdale

Springdale along with Bentonville, Rogers and Fayetteville comprise the four cities that comprise NWA. With a population of 69,797, according to the 2010 Census, Springdale is the fourth largest city in Arkansas. Springdale is headquarters to Tyson Foods, Inc., the largest meat producing company in the world and it is also the headquarters of Fuels & Supplies, the leading fuel supplier of NWA.

Arts

Arts Center of the Ozarks
214 South Main
Springdale, AR 72764
Phone: (479) 751-5441

Established in 1967, the Arts Center of the Ozarks offers opportunities for all creative outlets including: singing, painting, dancing, acting, music and sewing. The Center is known as the heart of the arts in NWA. Its goal is to make terrific entertainment while providing excellent educational opportunities in the arts. The hands-on approach to arts utilizes creative inspiration and provides amazing surprises for the entire family.

Shiloh Museum of Ozark History
118 West Johnson Ave
Springdale, AR 72764
Phone: (479) 750-8165

The Shiloh Museum of Ozark History focuses on the history of the Northwest Arkansas Ozarks. It got its name from the pioneer community of Shiloh, which later in the 1870s became known as Springdale.

At the museum, is a research library, which houses a collection of over 500, 000 pictures of the Ozarks. Also on the grounds are six historic buildings, which highlight the lives of the ordinary people who lived in the rural communities of the Ozarks. Additionally, there are also many permanent exhibits portraying the lives of these everyday men, women and children.

Dining in Springdale

Fine Dining
James at the Mill

American
Spring Street Grill
Market Place Grill
Neil's Cafe
Wagon Wheel Country Café
Blue Monkey Grill

Asian
Pattaya Thai Sushi
Mama Tang
Blufin Sushi Bar Japanese Grill
Thai Secret
Silk Road Restaurant
Venesian Inn

Breakfast
Susan's Restaurant (Great Breakfast)
Neil's Cafe
Waffle Hut Family Restaurant
Cracker Barrel Old Country Store

Italian
Joe's Pizza & Pasta Italian Grill
Mama Z's Cafe
Guido's Pizza

Mexican
Flying Burrito

Hotels in Springdale

Luxury

Inn at the Mill, an Ascend Collection Hotel
Doubletree Club by Hilton

Mid-Range Accommodations

Fairfield Inn Suites
Laquinta Inn & Suites
Comfort Suites
Sleep Inn Suites

B&B

Magnolia Gardens Inn

Sports & Recreation

Image credit Arkansas.com

Arvest Baseball Park - Home of The Arkansas Naturals
Corner of 56th and Watkins
3000 South 56th Street,
Springdale, AR 72764
Phone: (479) 927-4900

The Northwest Arkansas Naturals baseball team calls the Arvest Ballpark its home. In the summer, the ballpark is the exciting venue for 70 home games, which provide excellent high quality entertainment for the entire region. The ballpark also hosts a variety of other activities including fairs, car shows and festivals.

All Star Sports Arena
1906 Cambridge Street
Springdale, AR 72764
(479) 750-2600

The All Star Sports Arena in Springdale is a multiple use facility offering basketball/volleyball courts, martial arts, wrestling, youth flag football, cheerleading and dance studios and an all-female roller derby.

This 130,000 square foot sports complex also offers various adult and youth sport leagues.

Jones Center for Families
922 East Emma Avenue
Springdale, AR 72756
(479) 756-8090

The Jones Center is a fantastic multiple purpose center for NWA. It includes an indoor swimming pool, fitness center, gymnasium with a volleyball and basketball court, an ice rink, track, a community park and showers and locker rooms.

In addition to recreational opportunities, the Center has a teen center, an on-site chapel and a facility for genealogy research. There are also ongoing programs for kids, teens, families and seniors. Admission and all activities and classes are free at the Center.

Springdale Country Club
Designed by Bland P. Pittman and opened in 1927, the 18-hole course at Springdale Country Club offers plenty of golf. The course features 6,673 yards of golf from the longest tees for a par of 72. The course rating is 72.1 and it has a slope rating of 119.

Rodeo of the Ozarks
1423 E. Emma Ave.
Springdale, AR 72764
Phone: (479) 756-0464

Named one of the top 5 Large Outdoor Rodeos in 2011 by the PRCA, the Rodeo of the Ozarks brings the best of cowboys and stock together every year for some top level competition.

I hope you have enjoyed the information on Northwest Arkansas. If you would like additional information as well as restaurant and hotel discounts, please visit. http://annaseeger.blogspot.com/. If you have addition to be included in the next edition, please email us theannaseeger@gmail.com.

All the best,
Anna Seeger

www.ingramcontent.com/pod-product-compliance
Lightning Source LLC
Chambersburg PA
CBHW042309150426
43198CB00001B/19